THE KATHLEEN PARTRIDGE SERIES

Kathleen Partridge's Book of Flowers
Kathleen Partridge's Book of Friendship
Kathleen Partridge's Book of Golden Thoughts
Kathleen Partridge's Book of Tranquil Moments

First published in Great Britain in 1997 by
Jarrold Publishing Ltd
Whitefriars, Norwich NR3 1TR

Designed and produced by Visual Image, Craigend, Brimley Hill,
Churchstanton, Taunton, Somerset TA3 7QH

Illustrations by Jane Watkins

Edited by Donald Greig

ISBN 0-7117-0901-7

Copyright © Jarrold Publishing 1997

Printed by Proost, Belgium 1/97

Kathleen Partridge's
BOOK OF
Flowers

Kathleen Partridge

Stars of Spring

*Primrose, Star of Spring, a happy
heart I'll not deny you;
Welcome here! but I would rather
gather you than buy you.*

*It is my greatest pleasure to go seeking
in the dell,
To climb a bank and part the sturdy
leaves I love so well.*

*To hunt in quiet places where a stream
will play a tune
And a tiny posy represents a
well-spent afternoon.*

*Here's fragrance for the weary heart by
God Himself designed,
Because I gather peace with every
primrose that I find.*

Fairy Flowers

Perfect are the petals on a palette
leaf of green
Poised like fairy wings
embroidered for the fairy queen.
These cyclamens called
'diffident' are shy, but not
forlorn,
Shiny as the sunset and as
delicate as dawn.
Isn't it amazing how the petals
are uncurled,
To think that we awake to find
such beauty in the world!

Carpet of Blue

Bluer than a sailor's eyes
Bluer than the bluest skies
Spread your carpet, ring your bells
Round the trees and down the dells.

Call a meeting place for friends
In the woods where anger ends,
Tell two hearts for truelove's sake
To keep the loving vows they make.

Though trains may whistle, traffic roar
And aircraft in the heavens soar,
Though houses rise and cities fall
The bluebells grow in spite of all.

Wild Daffodils

Somewhere behind the country lanes, one
jump beyond the hedges,
There will be yellow daffodils with frilly
trumpet edges;
Somewhere beneath an ancient oak or just
below a stile,
There will be wild, sweet golden heads that
nod to hide a smile.

Though cities boast of barrows that are
selling daffodils,
And city workers buy a bunch to grace
their window-sills,
Yet people in the busy streets will walk
along unknowing
About the haunts in springtime where the
daffodils are growing.

Where Tulips Grow

To see a mass of tulips red
In any field or garden bed
Proud and upright, cool and clean
Folded round in wraps of green

Makes me see the world anew
In tones as loyal and as true
Where men uphold a friend and neighbour
And rest contented after labour.

Forget-me-not

How could I forget you
This flower that speaks your name,
Bonny, blue and beautiful
It always stays the same.

Dancing in a sweet warm world
Where views are tender green
Where days are fair and fragrant
And the twilight is serene.

Small and frail and lovable
How many hours you bless,
I look for you to borrow peace
Then share your happiness.

Roses, Roses
Everywhere

✤

In the heart of every rose
A pearl of dew prepares to settle,
Eternal summer lingers
In the texture of a petal.

A rose will grace a mansion
Her intrusion needs no pardon,
She is equally at home
In any little cottage garden.

✤

Old Fashioned Flowers

It's the old fashioned honeysuckle
The common hedgerow kind
That has the sweetest smell
And leaves a memory behind.

It's the old fashioned sweet peas
Like baby butterflies
That fill the room with fragrance
And entrance our waking eyes.

Island of Waterlilies

It was a most impressive sight –
Waterlilies on a lake,
Masses of them left and right,
Without a space, without a break.

You couldn't put a pin between,
So waxy-white and close were they,
An island for a fairy queen,
Where small immortal creatures play.

Where sparrows perch on floating leaves
And sing for joy and beauty's sake,
To think a world that toils and grieves
Grows waterlilies on a lake.

Buttercups and Daisies

The buttercup is dressing in a shade that
suits her well –
The same sweet yellow that she wore when
she was last year's belle.

The daisy still appears in white, but blushes
when she's shy,
And seems to fit the fashion as the different
years go by.

The same clothes suit the self-same flowers
while 'new looks' come and go,
Yet all occasions find the flowers dressed
perfectly on show.

Over the Wall

The clematis must climb the wall
To see the other side,
The hollyhocks are curious too
And rosebay has a lovely view
Outgazing far and wide.
Yet none of them will beg your pardon
When they peer into your garden
Always reaching for a better view;
Such saucy flowers, although not ours,
'I'd love some in my garden… Wouldn't you?'

Last to Reign

The queen of all the gardens there she stands
While Autumn tints the world with golden hands,
Reigning alone, the dahlia rules the world
With buttons, pompons or with spikes uncurled.

And there are some that rule, as if in state,
With blossoms like a giant golden plate
And those with ragged curls that sweetly swing
As if to give the earth her final fling.

Autumn Flowers

This is the season of views that are golden,
Of trees that are burnished and leaves edged with
gilt,
Sunflowers, dahlias, yellow and shining,
And hedges where splashes of varnish are spilt.

This is the season of red-gold and spun-gold,
Of rosy-gold creeper and coppery fern,
Of wealth in the byways and gleams in the meadow,
Of old-gold and pale-gold wherever we turn.

Chrysanthemums

Chrysanthemums are always here when
other flowers wane,
Shaking out their ragged petals in a
shower of rain.

Theirs is not a fleeting visit like a gust of
air
As if they had no time and must be
rushing off elsewhere,
But quite a lengthy stay, so gold, so
gracious, so serene,
Fetching warmth and beauty into
nature's fading green.

Chrysanthemums, the winter wonders,
full of courage, full of cheer,
When other flowers pass, then they are
waiting in the rear.

Winter Flowers

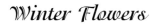

Where paths are frosty, woods are wet
I haven't seen a snowdrop yet
But am enjoying the sensation
Of living in anticipation.

One day when the snow is shrinking
And I am glancing down unthinking
There will be snowdrops, white and sweet
Encased in green about my feet.

And if by chance the time is right
To find a winter aconite
Then will I say with words sincere
'O what a happy time of year'.

Nicknames

The nicknames of the flowers
Must be as old as father time,
Pert, appealing, pretty
Set to music and to rhyme.

Thrift and grannies bonnet,
Rose of Sharon, meadow rue,
Jacob's ladder, creeping Jenny,
Shepherd's needle, bird's-eye blue.

Who named the thyme and tonguebleed,
Old man's beard, and dragonwort,
And set the ragged robin
Next to break your mother's heart?

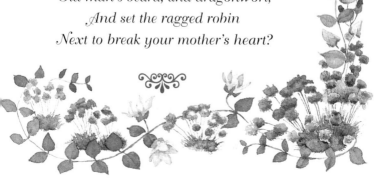

Wallflowers

'Wallflower'! What a clumsy name for
petals velvet soft,
For perfume so exquisite that it carries
dreams aloft;
Glowing yellow, crimson red and russet
ringed with green,
Sturdy leaves to glimpse with fragrant
mystery between.

'Wallflower'! Had the donor of this name
no admiration
For blooms that race the spring and beat
it to its destination?
Why not a name of glory and of beauty
bravely drawn
From sounds as soft as sunset, and as
rich as crimson dawn.

Wisdom from Flowers

The snowdrops have died on the bank by the river,
But as they were fading the crocuses grew;
I remember the scene, bright with yellow and mauve,
When it seemed but a day since the white held the
view.

And just as I mourned that the crocus was over,
The tips of the hyacinth broke through the bed,
Followed by others in waxen perfection;
But now there are daffodils dancing instead.

I no longer sigh for the loss of a flower,
But look with expectancy into the grass;
God takes with one hand but gives with another,
Will there be tulips the next time I pass?